To panda girl

Why is Panda Fat?
Another Book of Haikus
© 2023 Nolen Lee

All rights reserved. Punching Pandas® and all characters are trademarks of Nolen Lee. No portion of this publication may be reproduced or transmitted in any form or by any means, without the express written permission of Nolen Lee. Names, characters, places, and incidents featured in this publication either are the product of the author's imagination or are used fictitiously. Any resemblance to actual persons (living or dead), events, or locales, without satiric intent is coincidental.

Why is Panda Fat? Another Book of Haikus | written and illustrated by Nolen Lee

Summary: The third installment of haikus and illustrations featuring Pak the punching panda and his pals. Featuring Petunia Panda, Jr. Panda, Pippa Panda, Grammy Panda, Randy the red panda, Topher the Akita dog, Chimu the calico cat, Nop the mallard duck, Summer the squirrel, Buxton the beaver, and Evil Steve the yellow-throated marten (actually he's not Pak's friend).

Published by
Punching Pandas, LLC.
First edition: August 2023
ISBN 978-0-9998235-5-2
punchingpandas.com

Why is Panda Fat?

Another Book of Haikus

Made by Nolen Lee

Punching Pandas®

Why is panda fat?

Because everyone has fat

Panda just has more

The key to wisdom

Is not knowing everything

It's having a beard

To remove a weed

Look for root and dig it out

And hope it's not deep

Teach panda to fish

Panda can eat for lifetime

Bite size may vary

Life is like donut

Soft and sweet with hole inside

Wait, now I'm hungry

Do not fear failure

For it is like a teacher

Who gives lots of F's

Like many chain links

Together we can do more

Unless links are weak

Focus on the goal

Ignore all the distractions

Wait... is that... bacon?

One stick can be snapped

But many are hard to break

Then use a big axe

In healthy debate

The best argument will win

This debate is ill

A family's bonds

There are none that are stronger

Except superglue

A hometown flavor

Brings back many memories

Of why it tastes gross

Honor your parents

Thank them for their sacrifice

Hey, did you hear me?

A mother who loves

Will give her all for her young

But she keeps her snacks

Listen to elders

For they know much about life

Except for malware

Laughter of children

Overflows with joy and life

And ruins my nap

The older sibling

Can teach the young what is good

And where cookies are

The caring father

Encourages and supports

By yelling a lot

Sharing is caring

Better to give than receive

But not when it's germs

Why is panda fat?

Who gets to decide what's fat?

Is it fat police?

Tiny drops of rain

Softly they pitter patter

Now where is that leak?

The mighty bamboo

It stands against all forces

Not so with panda

A pebble's ripples

Can cross over a whole pond

Is it lunch time yet?

Watch the busy ants

Though small,
 they are hard workers

Go work somewhere else!

In times of trouble

First, be calm and collected

And then you panic

Curious children

Will ask many a question

And ask, and ask, and...

Love is like diamond

So many ways it can shine

And way too pricey

The path to goodness

Is narrow and difficult

So travel by air

Embrace quiet times

Silence brings clarity and...

Hey! Get back to bed!

Why is panda fat?

Maybe ask different question

Why panda handsome?

Live a simple life

Don't fret over possessions

For kids will break them

Precious are skilled hands

They solve many a problem

Except saggy pants

The creative mind

It feeds on inspiration

And makes "art," I guess…

What makes a hero?

Honor, courage, selflessness

And useful powers

Fool me, shame on you

Fool me twice,
          then shame on me

Stop with the fooling!

Cooperation

One must be a team player

And not a ball hog

A patient teacher

Over time cares and nurtures

And longs for the bell

The youth of today

Will be tomorrow's leaders

Oh boy, are we doomed

The innovator

Can make a great idea

And lots of big duds

So why panda fat?

Panda now has the answer

It is because… Zzz…

Punching Pandas® was created by the hooman Nolen Lee, who does whatever panda tells him. He wrote "The Panda is Fat," in 2018 and "The Panda is Still Fat" in 2019 which gave him the idea to write this book. He resides in the Seattle area and is under constant surveillance by his wife and two kids.

 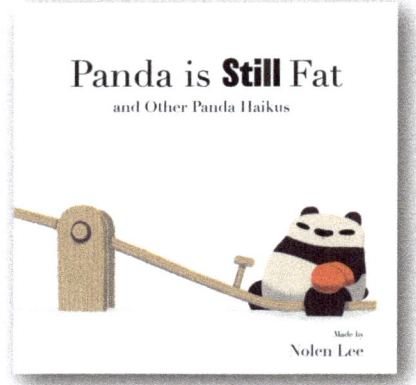

These are the other two panda books if you can't get enough of panda haikus. Available at bookstores. Beware.

Visit panda and friends at
punchingpandas.com

www.ingramcontent.com/pod-product-compliance
Lightning Source LLC
Chambersburg PA
CBHW061157010526
44118CB00027B/3001